monday morning®

ABC Art

by Marilynn G. Barr

Publisher: Roberta Suid
Editor: Carol Whiteley
Production: Susan Cronin-Paris

Monday Morning is a registered trademark of
Monday Morning Books, Inc.

Entire contents copyright © 1989 by Monday Morning
Books, Inc., Box 1680, Palo Alto, California 94302

ISBN 0-912107-97-9

Printed in the United States of America
9 8 7 6 5 4 3 2 1

TABLE OF CONTENTS

INTRODUCTION

ABC Art is an ABC skills book for pre-kindergarten and kindergarten children. It's an idea-packed resource that contains alphabet letter cards and picture cards, plus suggestions for hands-on activities and art projects, such as books, mobiles, banners, and more, that reinforce ABC skills. Multi-sensory experience in learning the alphabet is emphasized.

Four hands-on bulletin board activities are included in ABC Art. Large block letters are provided for these activities and others, and a "Super ABC" award is provided to present to children as they master skills (see page 12).

Skill Reinforcement

For kinesthetic-auditory experience, provide activities to help the children relate the letter name to its shape. Letters can be written on the board in large manuscript printing, and the children can take turns tracing each letter with chalk. Have the children name each letter as they trace. Children at their seats can trace paper patterns with their fingers or large crayons or pencils. They may also write or trace letters in trays of sand, salt, or gelatin.

Finger paint and pudding mix are other fun mediums for writing, as are clay and play dough for modeling.

For sound-symbol association, say the name of a picture to associate the sound for the letter. Have the children repeat the name and the initial sound. Encourage them to elicit as many words as they can for the sound of the letter. Their words may be listed on a chart for the children to illustrate. Pictures that match the initial sound can be cut out and pasted onto a chart for each letter. Objects that begin with the same sound can be collected and labeled with the matching letter.

For visual discrimination and auditory reinforcement, write three different letters on the chalkboard. Have one child come to the board. The teacher names one of the letters. The child points to the correct letter or writes it in the air and names it. Then have the child trace the letter with chalk, naming it again. Children at their seats can trace and name paper letter patterns or large embossed or felt letter cut-outs. For auditory input for the sound, say the sound for one of the letters on the board, for example, /a/ as in apple. Have the child find, trace, and name the letter. Key words can be given for added support.

Enrichment Activities

The enrichment activities are designed to give children more experience and practice with the alphabet. The activities are flexible and can be integrated within the curriculum and school day.

ABC Sorting–

Give each child a cup of alphabet macaroni and have the children sort the letters into jar lids or egg cartons labeled with the letters of the alphabet. Then have them paste the matching macaroni onto large letters as in ABC Collage Letters or they can make name cards for their desks. They can make words and paste them on construction paper leaves and pin or paste them onto a large green "word tree."

ABC "Show Me"–

Have the children place the small letter cards on their desk in alphabetical order. Ask them to show you a card by saying, "Show me T." When they hold up the correct card, reinforce their response by holding up your card and asking them to do a self-check. You may also ask for a letter by giving the sound—"Show me the letter for the sound /t/." A series of words may also be given for a letter the children must identify.

ABC Mystery Letter–

Have the children each select a mystery card from their small letter card set and turn it over or put it into their desk to keep it secret. Choose one child to come in front of the class with his or her mystery card held face down. Then let the class ask questions that will help them identify the mystery letter. The questions can be about the sound, name, or shape of the letter. Allow only five questions each time so that everyone gets a chance to have the mystery card discovered.

ABC Letter of the Week–

Each week, feature an alphabet letter and gear classroom experiences around it. For example, during "J Week" have the children make jello, play with jump ropes, wear jeans to school, eat jam sandwiches, and so on. At the end of the week, have the children take the large letters home and look for objects that start with that letter. You can also create a Letter of the Week bulletin board. Each week, enlarge and duplicate a letter card and picture cards for the letter of the week and pin them to the bulletin board.

ABC Go Fish Game

Two children can play this card game. Begin by shuffling a set of picture cards and placing them in a pile. Have each child take three cards from the pile to start. Then have one child take a card from the other child and see if the initial sound of the picture matches a card in the first child's hand. If it does, that player gets another turn. If cards don't match, the player "fishes" from the pile. If the card from the pile makes a match, the player gets another turn. The player who ends up with the most matches wins.

ABC Parade

Tape the large letter patterns to yard-sticks or dowels for children to hold while marching in order to the ABC song. After-wards, each child can present something that relates to his or her letter—a song, a story, a list of words, a jingle, a picture, an object, or an action.

ABC Flashcards

The small letter cards can be used as flashcards at school or at home. A member of the family can flash the cards in mixed order for the child to name the letter, or the child can look at the cards in order for further reinforcement and self-checking. When the sounds for the letters have been learned, they can be said when the cards are shown.

ABC Matchmates

Start this guessing game by making two sets of the large pattern letter cards. Then safety pin a letter to the back of each child's shirt or sweater, making sure that two of each letter are in circulation. Se-cretly tell each child what his or her letter is, and then have the children walk around, looking for the letter that matches their own. When a letter match is made, let the children color and decorate their letters.

ABC Hot Card

Glue the large letter patterns onto oak-tag. Ask a child to pick one of the letters to be the "hot" letter. Then have the children stand or sit in a circle and pass all the letters around the circle. The children will want to pass the "hot" letter on as quickly as possible so they don't get "burned." After a few moments, call out "Stop!" Ask the child holding the "hot" card to identify the letter, and then sit down in the middle of the circle. Have another child choose a new "hot" letter, and let play continue until five players are sitting inside the circle.

ABC Feely Box

Cut out the large block letters and glue them onto oaktag. Place them in a box with a hole big enough for a child's hand and the letter patterns to fit inside. Place a set of duplicate patterns on a nearby table. Have the first child reach into the box without looking, pick up and feel a letter, and try to guess what the letter is. Then have him or her take out the letter and match it to the appropriate pattern on the table. Two children can play at a time, seeing how many letters they can identify.

by Lillian Lieberman

Lillian Lieberman is a learning specialist and tutor for learning-disabled students, preschool to high school.

MAKING THE ABC ART

To use the ABC letters, review the name, shape, and sound for each letter. Have the children color the alphabet sheets, then paste them onto construction paper or oaktag. To use the ABC picture cards, have the children paste them onto construction paper and cut them out. Work on only one sheet at a time.

ABC Mobiles

Punch a hole at the top and bottom of each ABC letter card and picture card. String a length of yarn or ribbon through the hole in one letter card and tie the card to a clothes hanger. Below the letter card, tie on picture cards that match the letter. Hang several strands on the hanger to balance. Place the completed mobiles on a clothesline stretched across the room for a colorful display.

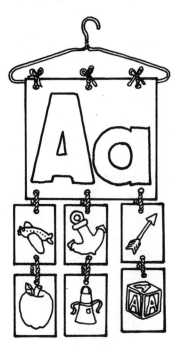

ABC Collage Letters

To make collages, trace the large block letters onto oaktag. Have each child cut out a letter and decorate it by pasting on an item that matches the letter. For example, seeds can be pasted all over the S, beans can be pasted on the B, pieces of a quilted material can be put on the Q. Keep the completed letters in a shoe box for study.

ABC Books

To make ABC books, have the children color the letters and cut them out, then paste each upper- and lower-case set on a sheet of construction paper. Staple the sheets together in book format and slip a length of colored yarn or ribbon through holes you punch at the top. The children can practice their ABC's by going over their book individually, with a partner, or in unison as a class. The books can be used later in bulletin board activities, or taken home for additional practice or to share with family.

ABC Banners

To make these banners, have the children paste a set of ABC letter cards on a very long piece of paper in alphabetical order. The banner can be rolled up to take home and share or display, or it can be used as a backdrop at a special ABC party parents are invited to. Poems, stories, plays, or songs that match the letters can be presented at that time, and alphabet cookies can be offered for refreshments.

BULLETIN BOARDS

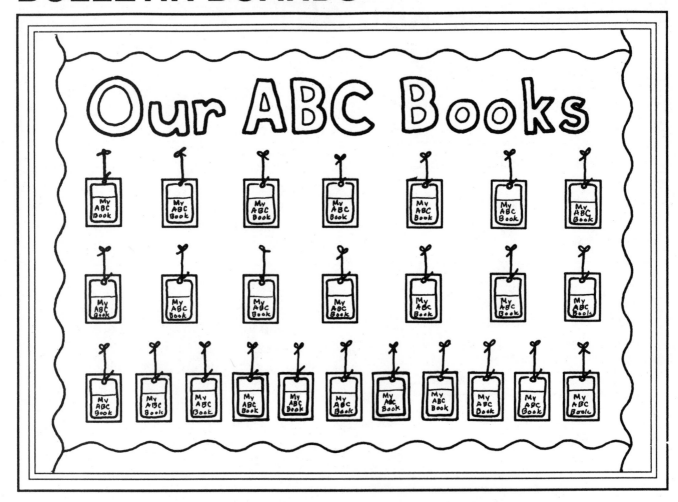

Our ABC Books

Enlarge and duplicate the large letters for the bulletin board title OUR ABC BOOKS. Duplicate the small letter cards and picture cards for each letter and the booklet cover provided here. Have the children color, cut out, and punch holes at the top of each card, including the cover. Bind the booklets with yarn and display them on the bulletin board.

8

ABC Zoo

Enlarge and duplicate the large letters to make the bulletin board title ABC ZOO. Then make bars for the zoo with yarn and pins. Duplicate the lower case letters and enlarge the zoo keeper. Pin the letters in between the bars in ABC order. Pin the zoo keeper to the side. Have the children color and cut out the ABC picture cards. Discuss the pictures and the initial letter and sound for each. Then have each child pin a picture by the matching letter to reinforce letter recognition and sound-symbol association.

Variation: Use the zoo animals from the picture cards. Use pictures from magazines or drawings of imaginary animals for letters not represented by an animal.

Our ABC Farm

Enlarge and duplicate the large letters for the bulletin board title OUR ABC FARM. Duplicate the lower case letters and enlarge the scarecrow. Outline the shape of a barn with yarn and pins. Then pin the letters to the barn and the scarecrow to the side. Have the children color and cut out the ABC picture cards. Discuss the pictures and the initial letter and sound for each. Have each child pin a picture by the matching letter to reinforce letter recognition and sound-symbol association.

Variation: Use the farm animals and objects from the picture cards. Use pictures from magazines or drawings of farm animals for letters not represented by an animal.

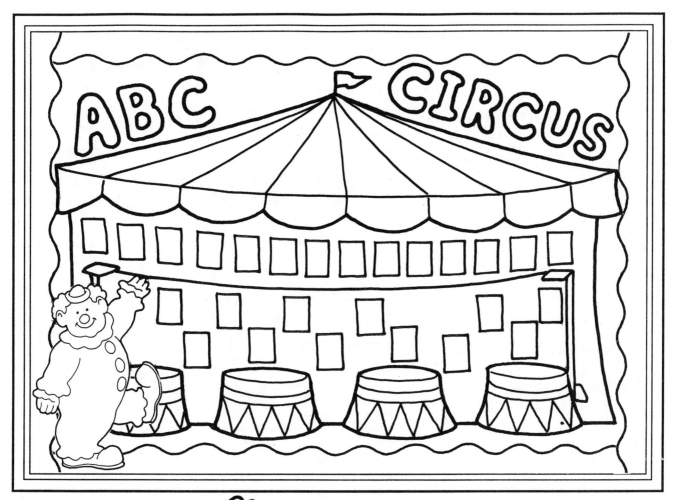

ABC Circus

Enlarge and duplicate the large letters for the bulletin board title ABC CIRCUS. Duplicate all the lower case letters and enlarge the clown. Outline the shape of a circus tent with yarn and pins and then pin the letters to the tent. Pin the clown to the side. Have the children color in and cut out the ABC picture cards. Discuss the pictures and the initial letter and sound for each. Have each child pin a picture by its matching letter to reinforce letter recognition and sound-symbol association.

Variation: Use the circus animals from the picture cards. Use pictures from magazines or drawings of circus animals and objects for letters not represented by an animal.

SUPER ABC AWARD

knows his/her alphabet.

Date and Signature

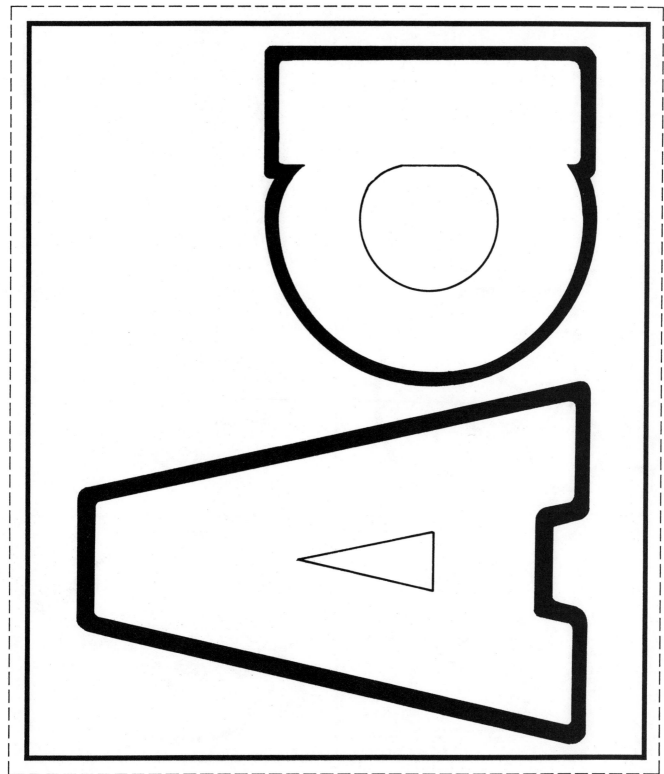

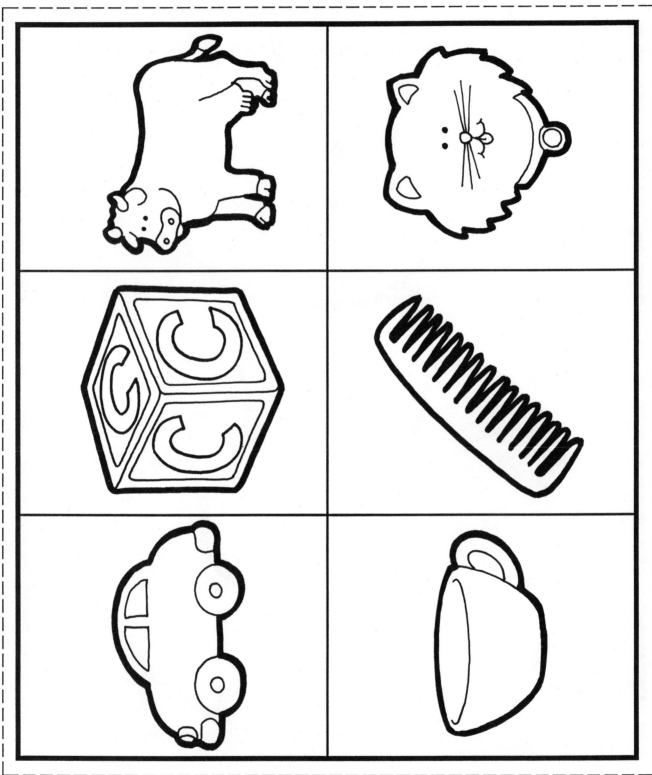

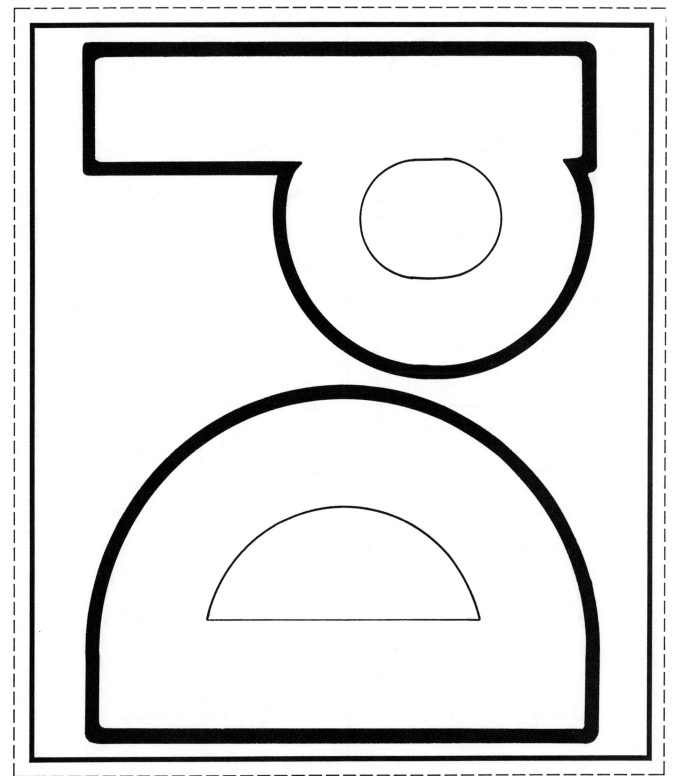

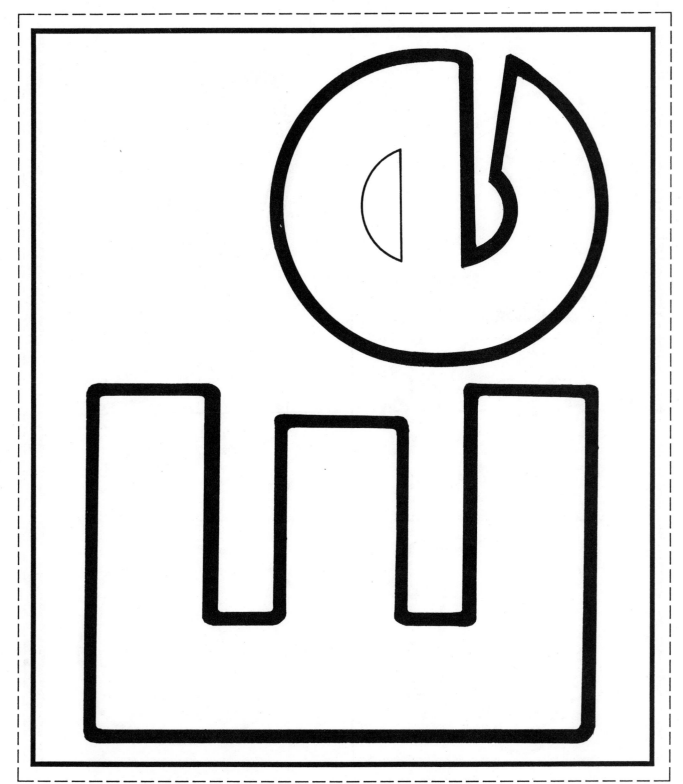

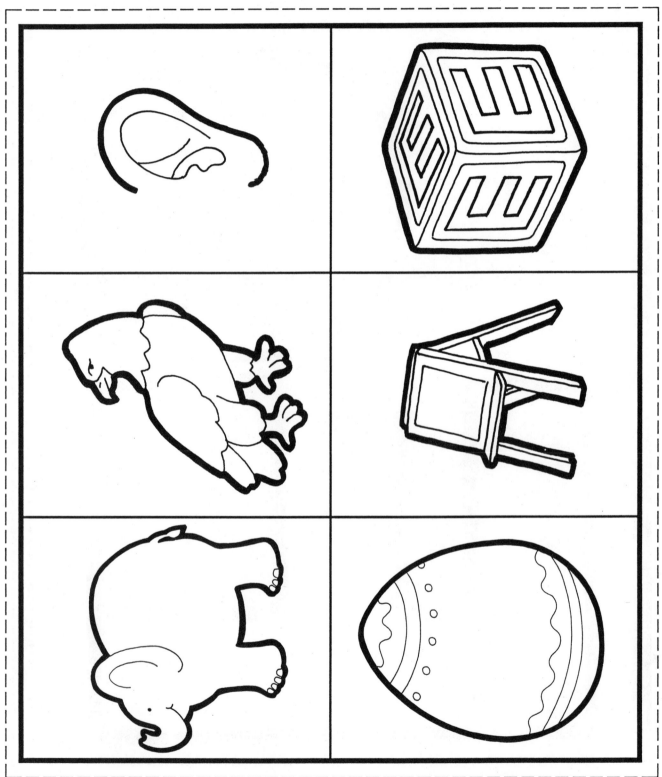

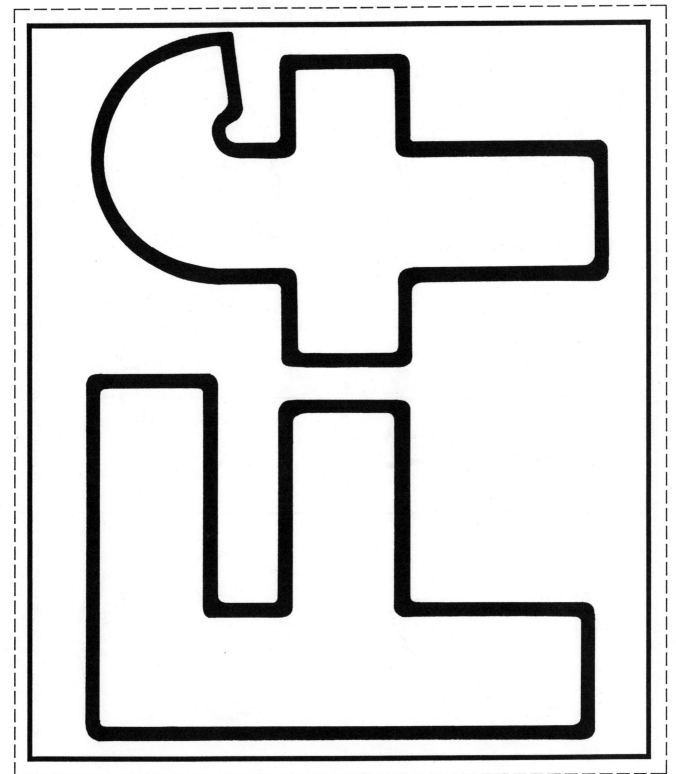

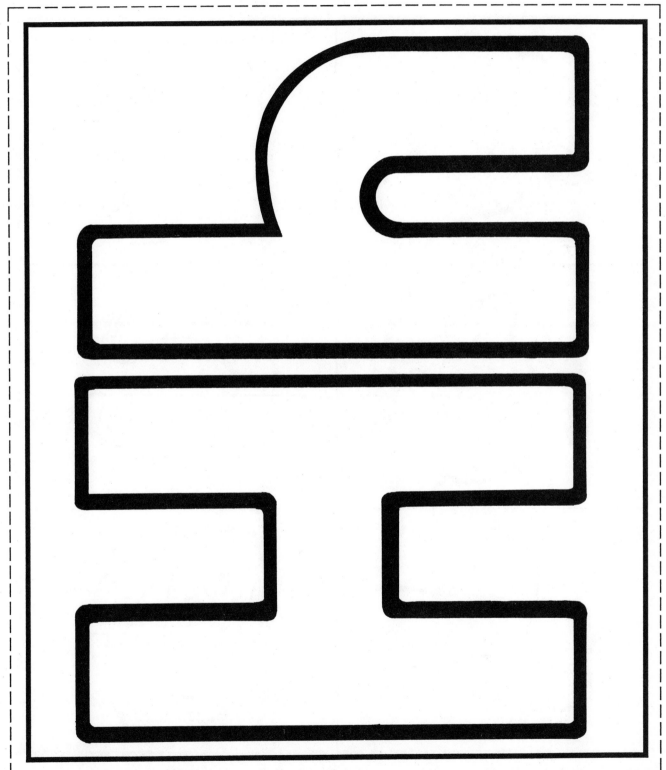

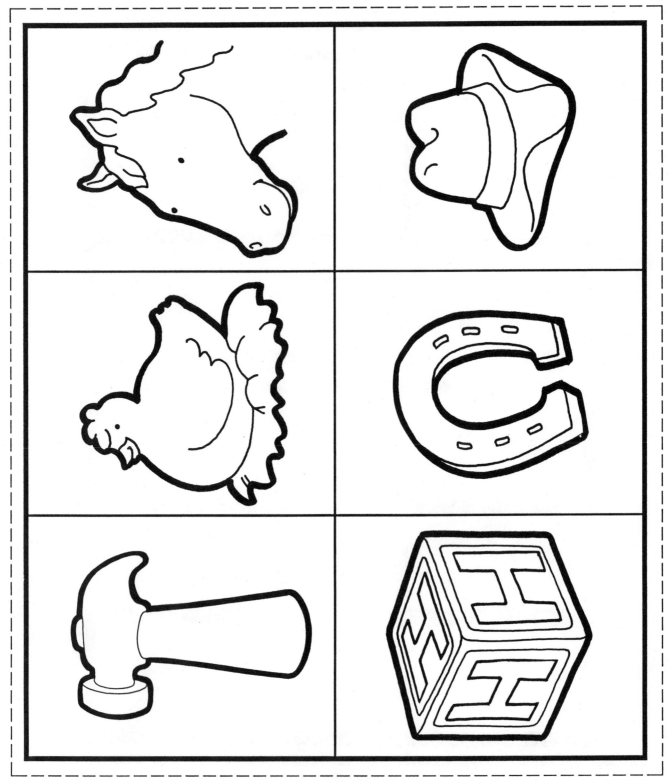

28

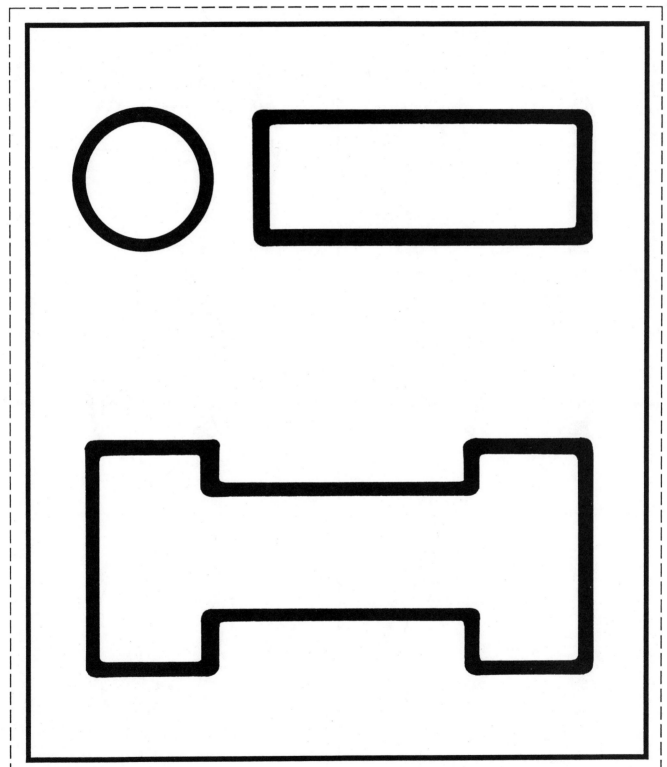

29

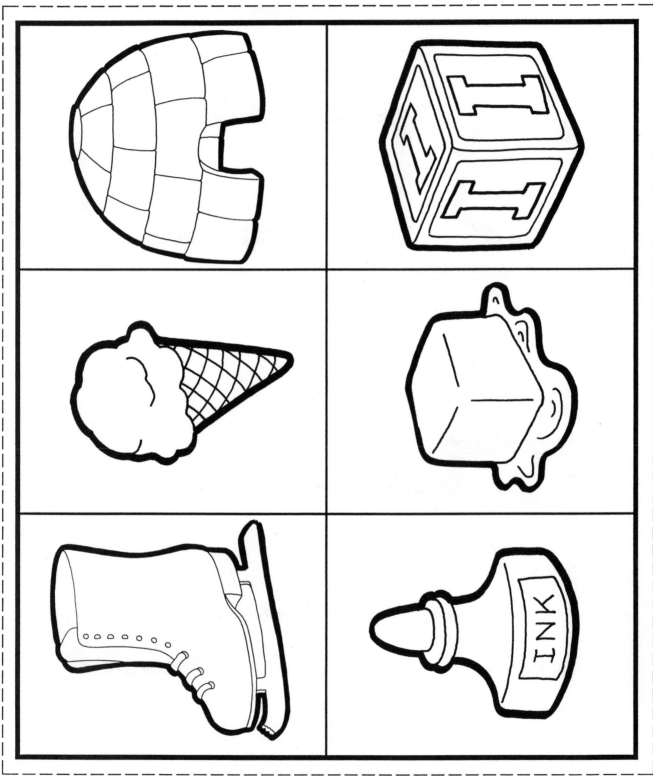

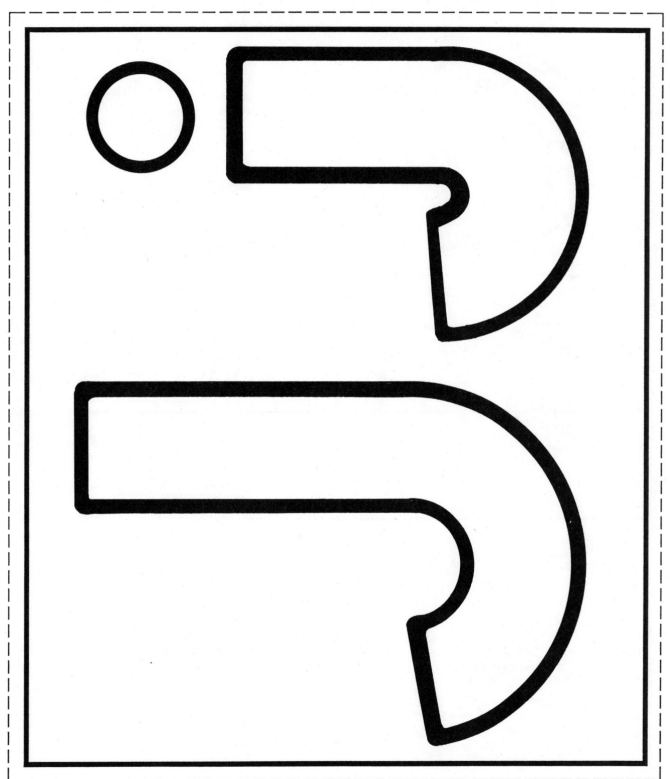

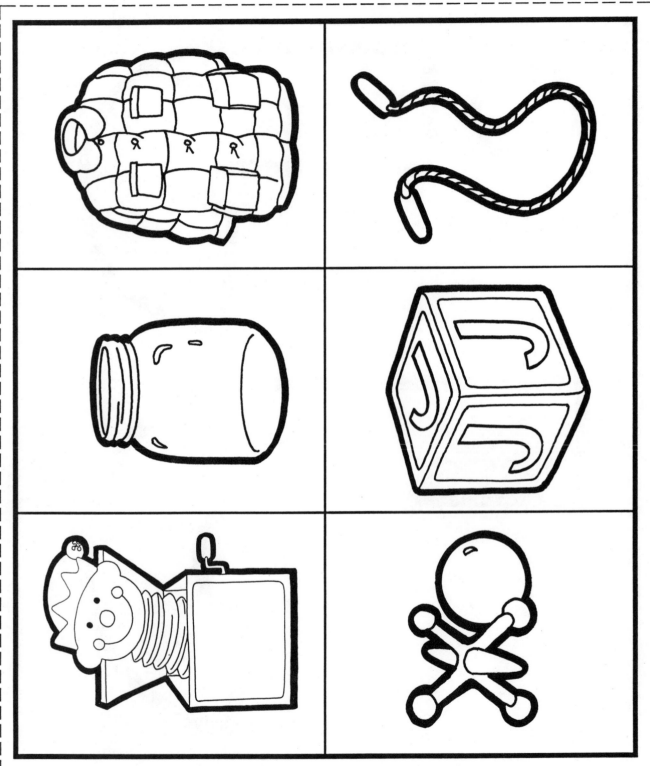

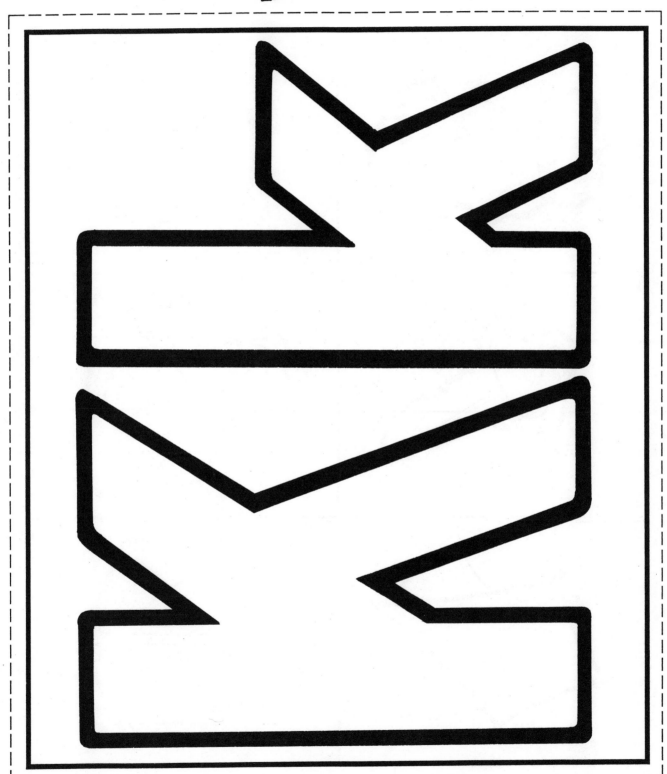

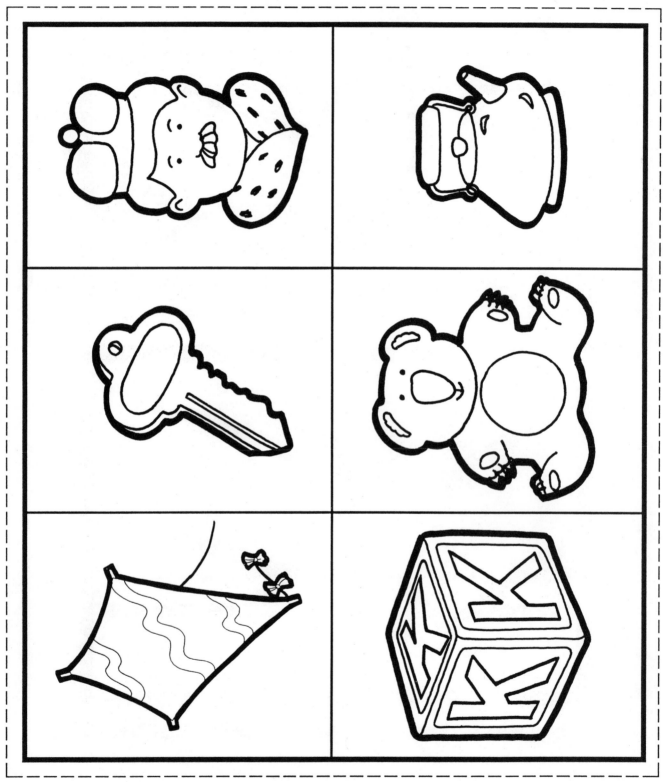

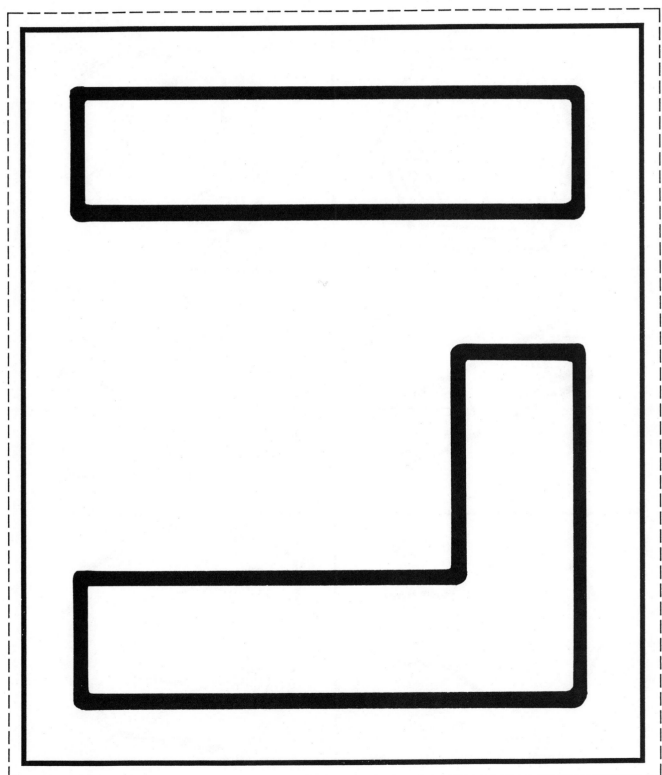

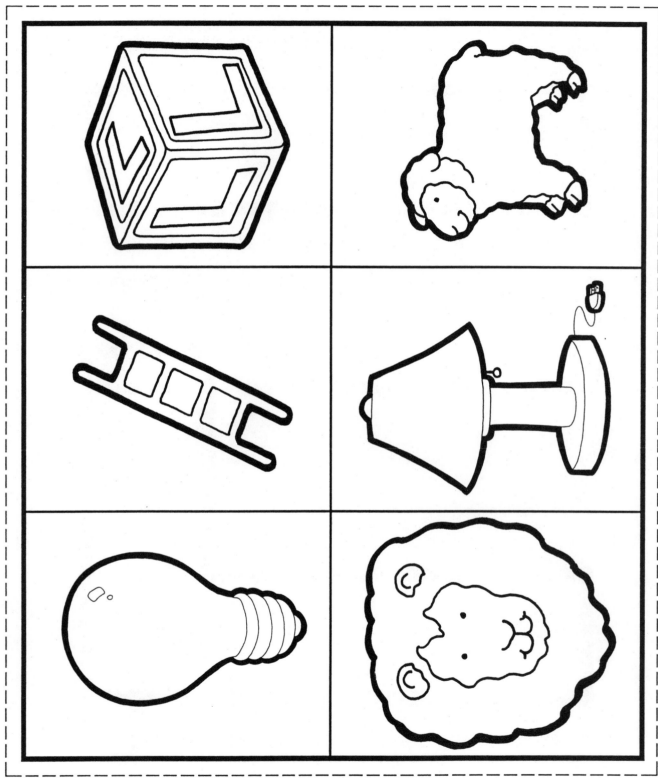

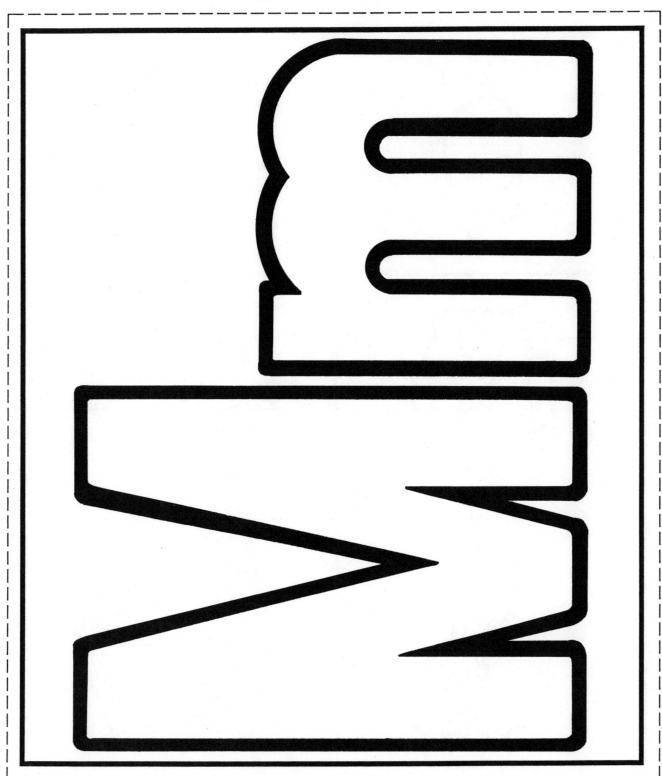

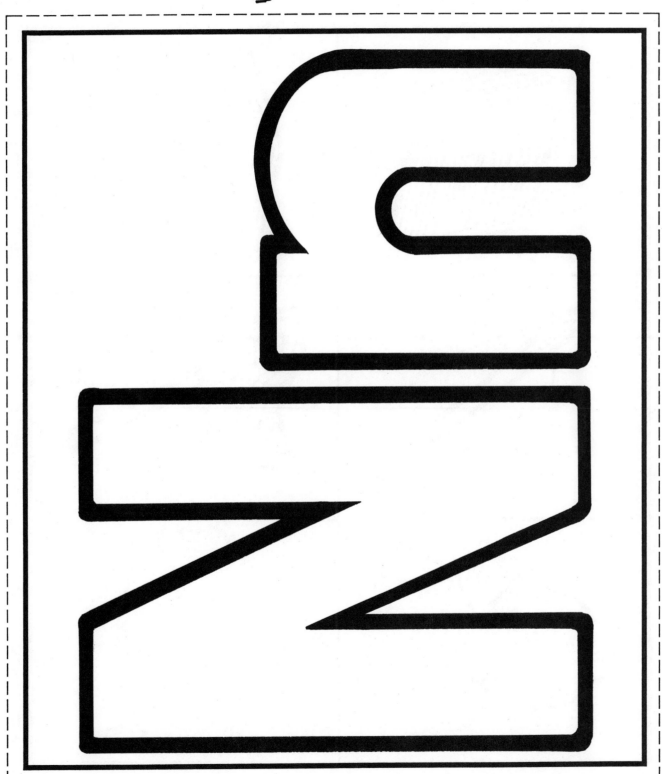

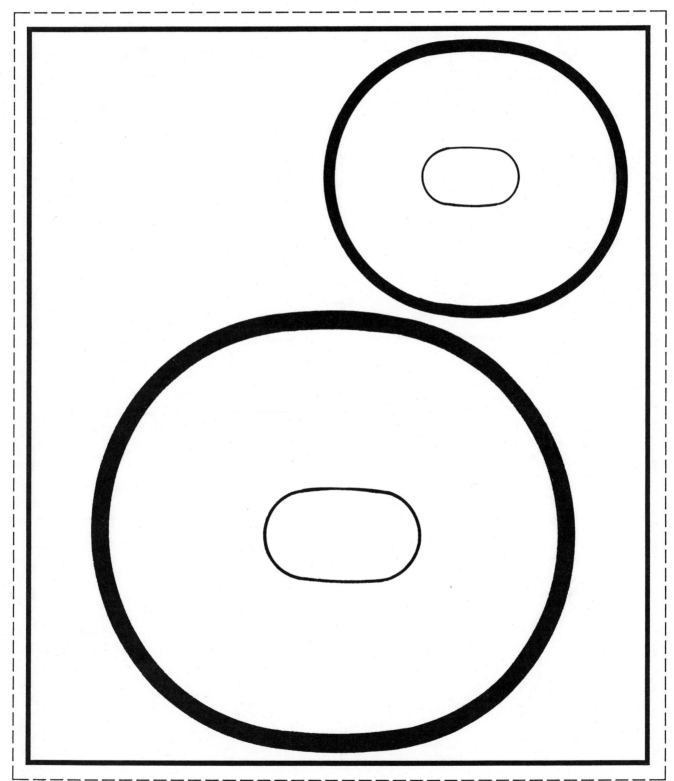

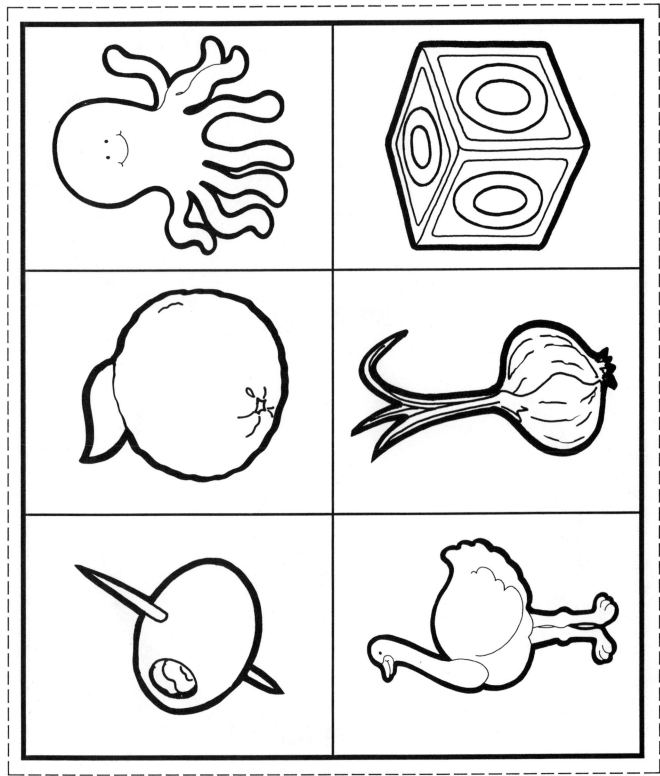

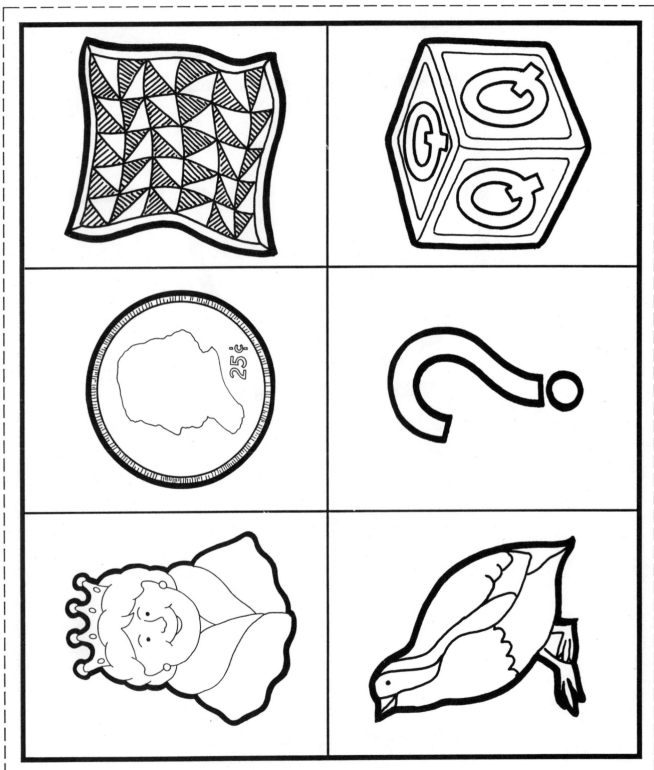

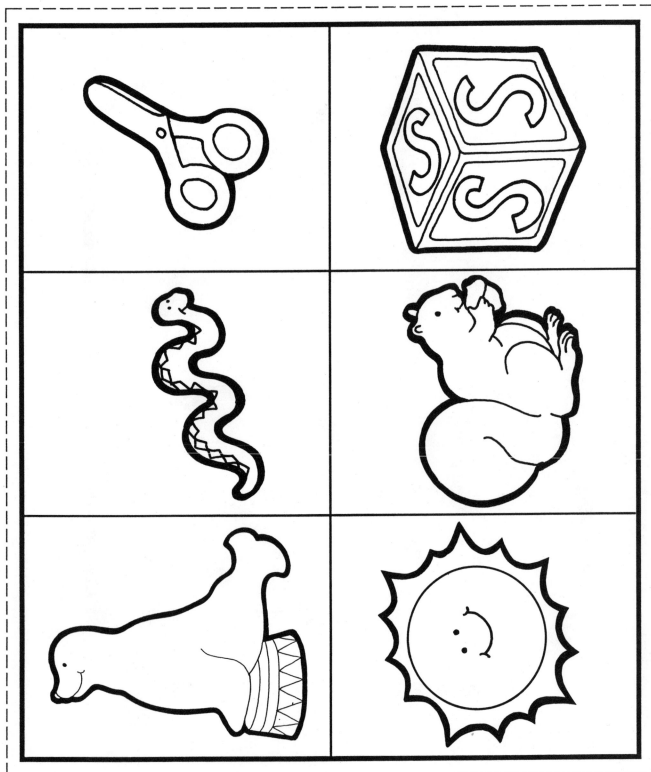

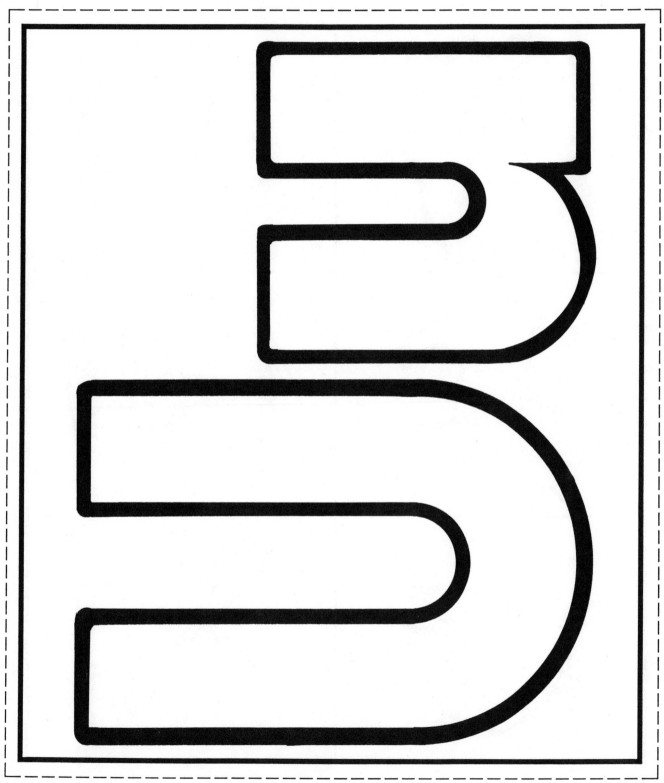

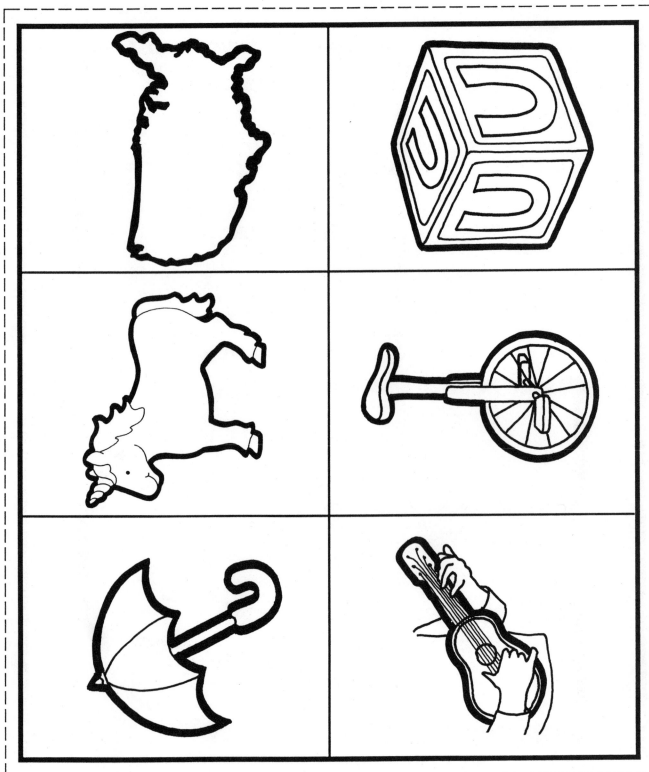

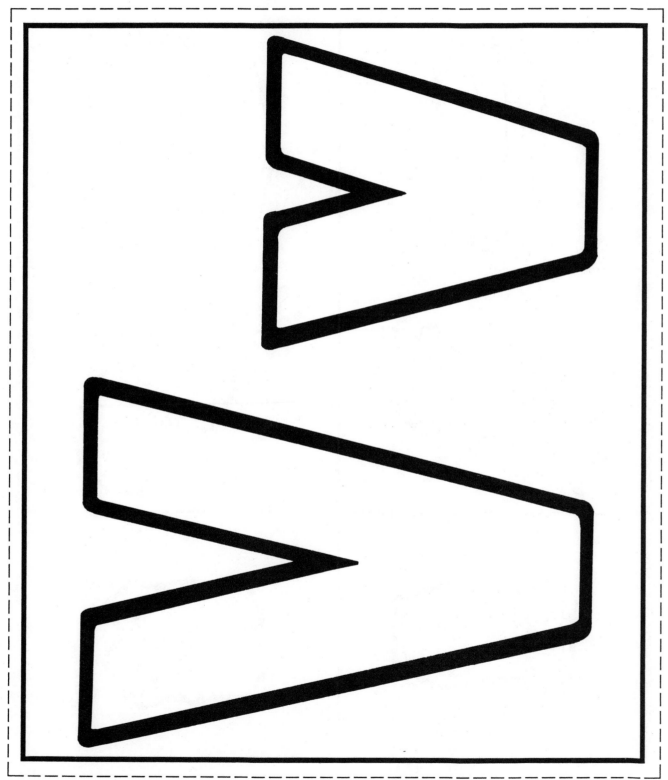

55

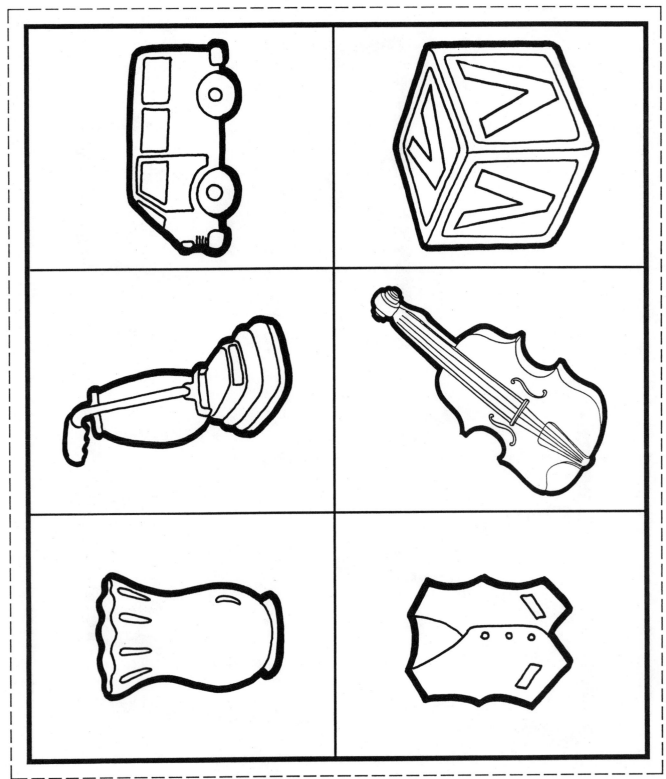

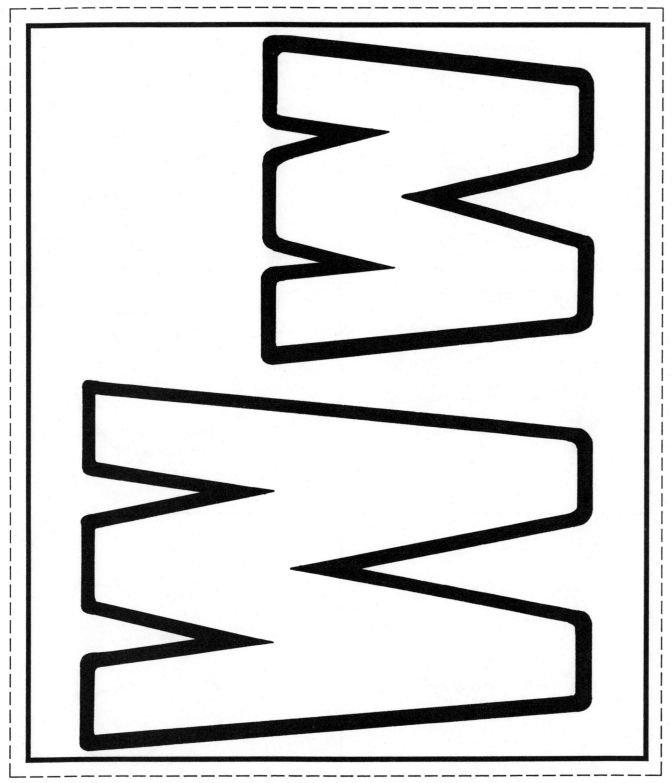

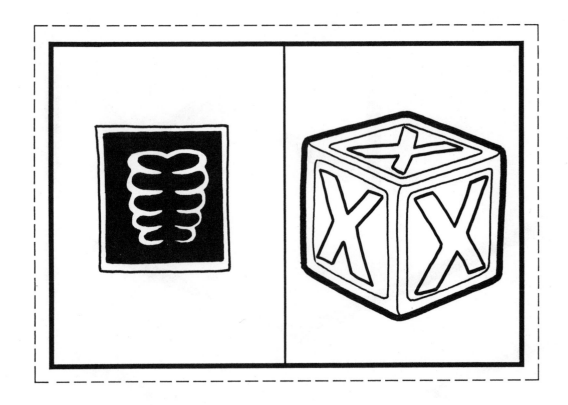

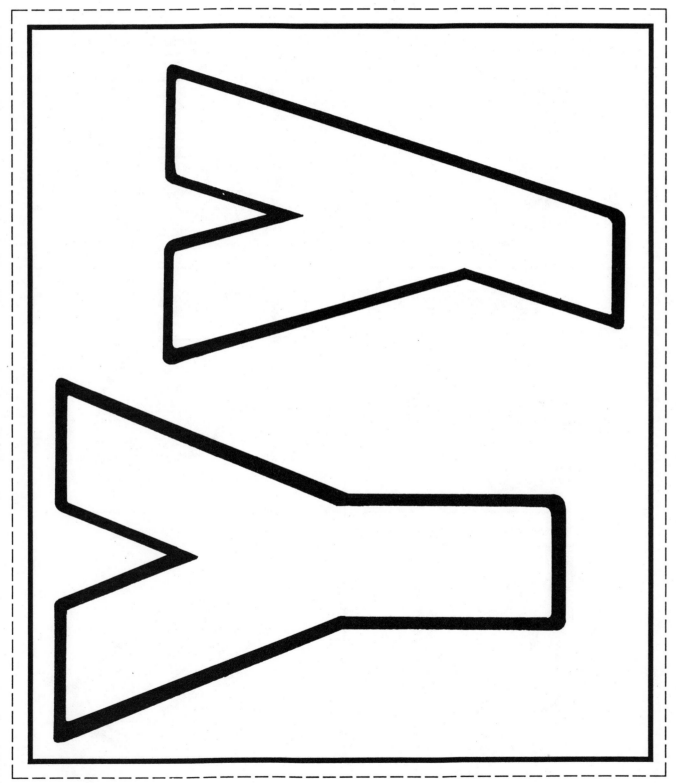

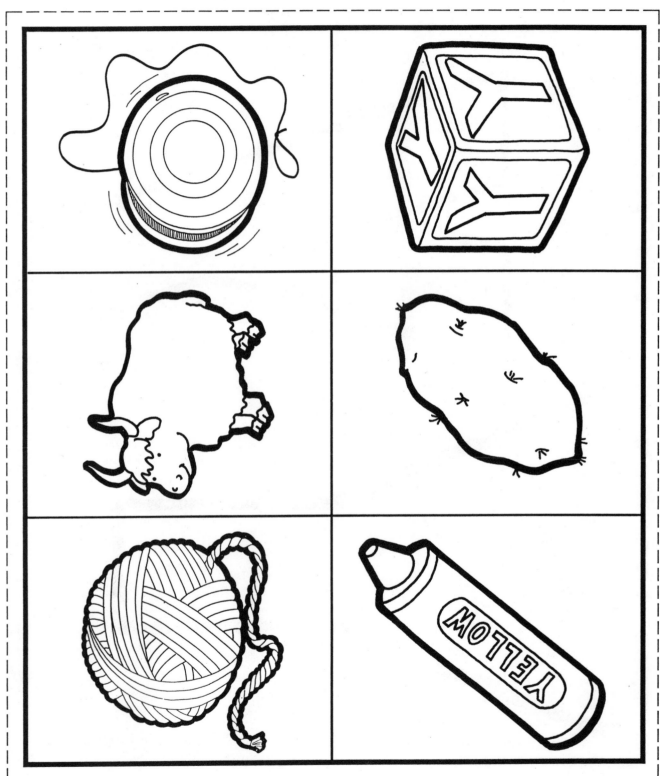

64